D1380791

*This delightful book is the latest in the series of Ladybird books which have been specially planned to help grown-ups with the world about them.*

*As in the other books in this series, the large clear script, the careful choice of words, the frequent repetition and the thoughtful matching of text with pictures all enable grown-ups to think they have taught themselves to cope. The subject of the book will greatly appeal to grown-ups.*

Series 999

# THE LADYBIRD
# BOOKS FOR GROWN-UPS SERIES

# THE EX

*by*

J.A. HAZELEY, N.S.F.W. and J.P. MORRIS, O.M.G.

(Authors of 'The Korean War In Pogs')

Publishers: Ladybird Books Ltd., Loughborough
*Printed in England. If wet, Italy.*

This is Tina with the man she used to call her husband.

Tina now calls this man "that man."

She also calls him "the most expensive mistake of my life" and other, much ruder things.

This man is Tina's ex.

Cherry tried telephoning Neil, but he had blocked her number.

Luckily, Neil's employer, the Merseyside Fire and Rescue Service, hasn't blocked her number.

At least, not yet.

The crash test dummy was invented in 1950 by Swedish engineer Ulrika Nordenstam. She modelled it in the likeness of her ex—husband, Vig.

Ulrika died in 1989 after a long battle with trying not to laugh.

Paul had never met Claire's new partner Harry before. Claire has gone to powder her nose and left them alone together.

"He's taller and younger than me," thinks Paul.

"Is that how bad I'll look after a few years with her?" worries Harry.

"Ah well," thinks Martin. "At least she left me a packet of cigarettes and a little bicycle made of pipe cleaners."

Matthew is troubled that Wyn still has a photo of his ex on his living room wall.

Wyn says it's not unreasonable. Most people have photographs of their former partners somewhere.

And it's only a metre and a half tall.

David had not seen Yvonne for ten years when he bumped into her near the watering–hole.

"I had forgotten how beautiful her skin is," he thinks to himself.

David is very sad.

"And if I don't put stamps on it, he'll have to pay at the other end?" asks Lucy.

"That's right, madam," says the man at the counter. "Is it a small packet or a parcel?"

"It's his drum kit," smiles Lucy. "And his skis. But I'm sending everything separately, so it's nineteen parcels in all."

With Lydia no longer in his life, Federico is spending some time going through his photo albums from the last twenty years and replacing her face with pictures of things he holds in higher esteem, like flint.

Nerina hopes Alwyn gets the message this time — and pretty soon, because she is worried she might sneeze and give the game away.

Since Phillip left him, Philip has had far more time for his Buxtehude.

Philip said Phillip didn't understand him.

Phillip said Philip wouldn't let him understand him.

In truth, nobody understands Philip, which is exactly how he likes it.

"Daddy says he's looking forward to having you for the weekend," Olivia tells Daisy and Noah.

"Is it this weekend?" asks Daisy.

"No," says Olivia, "it's not for a few months. Daddy's at an important sales conference."

"It's a very nice boat to have a sales conference on," says Noah, looking at the photo of Daddy with his new friend.

Cheryl was surprised by Steve's reaction to her proposal.

Ed and Natalie have remained friends since separating, and he often socialises with her and her new boyfriend, Zach. The three of them get along very well, and Ed gets to gaze into Natalie's blue eyes just like he used to when she looked at him that same way.

In ten years' time, this will form the basis of Ed's psychotherapy.

Jim is convinced that if Hazel can just be reminded of the smell of his after-shave, she will want him back.

Her holiday cottage is in sight.

"Plenty more fish in the sea," say all of Hugh's friends.

The sea is forty miles away. Hugh has not caught a thing.

Hugh is perfectly happy. To be honest, he has gone off fish.

Rocco paid a fortune for the website getdianeback.com but it failed to get Diane back.

So Rocco built a new Diane in his shed.

This Diane runs on a 1kW motor, can run most Android apps, and will probably not run off with Rocco's brother.

Troy meant to get off the tube at Liverpool Street, but he spotted his ex–girlfriend Jacinda at the other end of the carriage.

An hour and a quarter later, he tries not to be spotted as she gets off the train at Chesham.

The £85 taxi fare back into London is a small price to pay for glancing furtively from a distance at someone you have over 3,000 photos of, thinks Troy.

Though they separated some months ago, Oli and Matt are still partners in the lifesaving class they both attend.

Matt is good at pretending to be unconscious. He practised every night for the last year of their relationship.

Astronauts Deke Haldane and Nadia Amirkhanian were NASA's first astro-couple until they fell out on the launch pad and split up ten minutes after take-off.

To make matters worse, the third astronaut on the mission, Tiger Schlub, has a crush on Nadia.

Mission Control has no protocol for this in their flight plan. They have contacted Michelle Obama for advice.

As part of their divorce, Beth and Angus have carefully divided everything in two, so they both get a fair share of the house.

They have not yet talked about the boys.

Hassibullah thinks this statue he has made of his ex–girlfriend will win back her affections.

"Even though you've given her enormous lion's feet and smashed her nose off?" asks his friend.

"It's how I feel about her," says Hassibullah.

Adam still looks back on the thirty—five minutes he was probably Laura's boyfriend as the happiest of his life.

Three decades later, Adam's mother says it may be time he thought about moving on.

"It's just a trial separation," says Vanessa.

THE AUTHORS would like to record their gratitude and offer their apologies to the many Ladybird artists whose luminous work formed the glorious wallpaper of countless childhoods. Revisiting it for this book as grown-ups has been a privilege.

MICHAEL JOSEPH

UK | USA | Canada | Ireland | Australia
India | New Zealand | South Africa

Michael Joseph is part of the Penguin Random House group of companies whose addresses can be found at global.penguinrandomhouse.com

Penguin
Random House
UK

First published 2017
002

Copyright © Jason Hazeley and Joel Morris, 2017
All images copyright © Ladybird Books Ltd, 2017

The moral right of the authors has been asserted

Printed in Italy by L.E.G.O. S.p.A

A CIP catalogue record for this book is available from the British Library

ISBN: 978–0–718–18866–5

www.greenpenguin.co.uk